HAMLYN · COLOURFAX · SERIES

AMERICAN FOOTBALL

NEIL ROBERTSHAW

CONTENTS

HAMLYN

IN THE BEGINNING

American football came about partly by accident and partly by design. Its development from the soccer-based free-for-all, played by some American colleges more than a hundred years ago, to the highly disciplined contests played worldwide today, is a whistle-stop tour of some fascinating people, places and events.

THE EARLY DAYS

As far back as 1867, a rough-and-tumble kicking game was being played on the college campuses of north-eastern America to a set of regulations known as the Princeton Rules. By 1871, Harvard University was playing the "Boston Game", a version of the same game that allowed players to run with the ball. Boston-style football did become very popular but, in the early years, Harvard found opponents to be thin on the ground. One of their first, however, was a team from McGill University, from Montreal in Canada, who ventured south to Harvard on the May 15, 1874. This match was important as, had four of the team not fallen ill on the journey, American football might now feature 15 men on the field instead of 11. Two years later, five colleges decided on the rules for the first college football league, called the Intercollegiate Football Association.

THE ORIGINS OF GRIDIRON

In the next few decades, the game was changed completely and assumed some of the characteristics for which it is known today. During the 1880s, Yale University's Walter Camp, in many ways the father of the modern game, introduced

Right: *Playing kit has changed a great deal since the early days of American football. Even in the 1940s players wore woollen jerseys, and shoulder pads and helmets made of leather. There was little, or no strapping of joints and no protective face-cages.*

Right: *Today's player is altogether better protected. In addition to the rule changes which have made the game safer, modern footballers have the benefit of strong, lightweight padding and a specially-toughened helmet to prevent injuries.*

the "line of scrimmage", a "downs" system to determine possession of the ball, and the curious $53\frac{1}{3}$ yard (48.8 m) width of the field (he wanted to make the field wider in an effort to reduce the number of injuries suffered by the players, but this was as wide as Harvard's new stadium would allow!). In 1882, the game also became known as gridiron after he suggested drawing lines across the field at 5 yard (4.6 m) intervals to measure progress toward the goal-line. These markings gave the field a grid-like appearance and the nickname stuck.

Another great pioneer in the early days was Amos Alonzo Stagg, who was responsible for such important developments as the centre-snap, play-book, backfield shift and the huddle.

Changes such as these did little to reduce the game's risk of injury. In 1905, 159 players were seriously injured on the gridiron and 18 actually died. The American President, Theodore Roosevelt, intervened, insisting that the game "clean up its act" and become less violent. As a result, the National Collegiate Athletic Association was set up and the rules of American football were changed to ensure a safer game. This included the introduction of the forward pass which finally broke all the game's ties with rugby.

By 1912, American football had begun to look like the game that is now played in colleges and professional leagues throughout the world. In addition to the 13-man Canadian version, gridiron is now played in many European countries such as Italy, Finland, Great Britain and West Germany, and has taken root as far afield as Japan, New Zealand and Australia. American football, like the American hamburger, is well-travelled.

DOWN TO BASICS

THE FIELD

An American football field is 120 yards (109.7 m) long and 53⅓ yards (48.8 m) wide. At each end there is an area 10 yards (9.1 m) deep called an endzone, which is separated from the rest of the field by the two goal-lines. The field is marked at 5 yard (4.6 m) intervals by white lines that are called yard lines, and also at every 10 yards (9.1 m) by field numbers. Ten yards (9.1 m) behind each goal-line are a set of goal posts.

GAME TIME

The playing time of an American football game is one hour, divided into four quarters, each of 15 minutes. A game may actually last more than three hours, though, because the playing clock is stopped in certain situations, such as when a player goes out of bounds or when a pass is ruled incomplete.

THE TEAMS

There are two teams competing on the gridiron. Each team may consist of a roster of 45 players but only 11 are allowed on the field at any time.

SCORING

The idea of the game is to score more points than the opposing team. Points can be scored in several ways. Most valuable of all scores is the six-point touchdown where a player crosses his opponent's goal-line while in possession of the ball, or receives a pass through the air while standing in his opponent's endzone. Any team scoring a touchdown is then allowed to go for a conversion called an extra point attempt, worth one point. Usually, the scoring team will opt for a placekick – kicking the ball over the goal-line – and, if the ball passes through the goal posts and over the crossbar, it is awarded an extra point. Another type of scoring kick is the fieldgoal which can be attempted

from any distance and is worth three points. Finally, a team tackled in its own endzone gives away a two-point safety.

MOVING THE BALL

To score these points, the team in possession of the ball – the offense – must advance the ball toward its opponent's goal-line, either by running with it, passing it from one player to another or, in certain situations, kicking it from their hands (punting).

The offense is given four chances, or "downs", to gain 10 yards (9.1 m) on the field. If successful, they win the right to another four chances but, if not, they must hand the ball to their opponents. If on first down, the offense gains 3 yards (2.7 m), its position on the field as it goes into the next play is described as "second and seven" – it is on its second down and has 7 yards (6.4 m) to go.

The aim of the offense in most situations will be to reach another first down. The defense will be determined to stop them – and that's when all the fun starts.

Gridiron is not one long game from start to finish. It is broken up into sep-

---

PUNTING

Although, technically, a team has four downs in which to make 10 yards (9.1 m) it will rarely attempt to use more than 3. A team which has not been successful in moving the ball 10 yards (9.1 m) on its first three downs will usually use the fourth to kick the ball away, or, if in range of the goal posts, attempt a fieldgoal. By punting, the offense hands possession to the other team but ensures that it has to start its drive upfield from nearer its own goal-line. The job of kicking and punting – and defending against kicks and punts – is performed by a squad of players on each team called the special teams unit. The punter stands about 15 yards behind the scrimmage line. He catches the ball as it is snapped back by the center, steps forward while dropping the ball, and kicks it before it touches the ground.

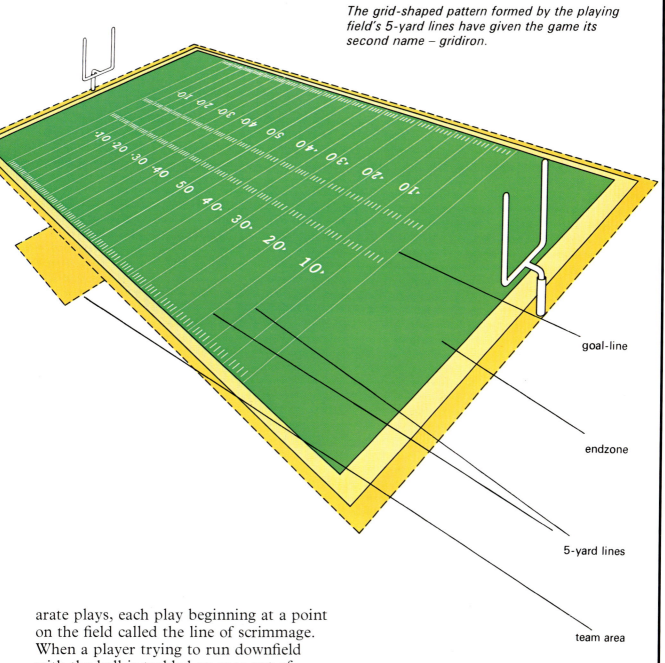

The grid-shaped pattern formed by the playing field's 5-yard lines have given the game its second name – gridiron.

goal-line

endzone

5-yard lines

team area

arate plays, each play beginning at a point on the field called the line of scrimmage. When a player trying to run downfield with the ball is tackled or goes out of bounds, the place at which he was stopped becomes the new line of scrimmage. Similarly, a player receiving a pass may then try to run with the ball and the place where his progress is stopped is the next line of scrimmage. However, if the ball touches the ground before a player catches it, the pass is said to be "incomplete", no yardage is gained and the ball goes back to the old line of scrimmage.

KEY TO THE DIAGRAMS

The following symbols and colours are used throughout this book. Defense is blue. Offense is gold. Key players are red.

defensive backs ●

linebackers ▼

defensive linemen ■

offensive players ●

center (offensive) ■

PROTECT AND SURVIVE

Before walking out on to the gridiron to do battle for the honour of his club, a player will put on up to 18 pieces of body armour weighing nearly 15 lb (6.8 kg). Playing on a hot day can add a further 3–4 lb (1–2 kg) worth of sweat.

STAGE ONE
The first layer consists of a cotton T-shirt, elasticated socks and a jock-strap.

Then the player tapes his ankles, knees and, later, hands, wrists and forearms, to protect the joints from sprains and reduce the impact of other types of injuries. Padding comes next in the form of a girdle with pockets into which hip, thigh and spine pads are inserted. Knee-pads and, sometimes, a steel knee-brace to protect the knees from a side-on tackle, are also strapped on.

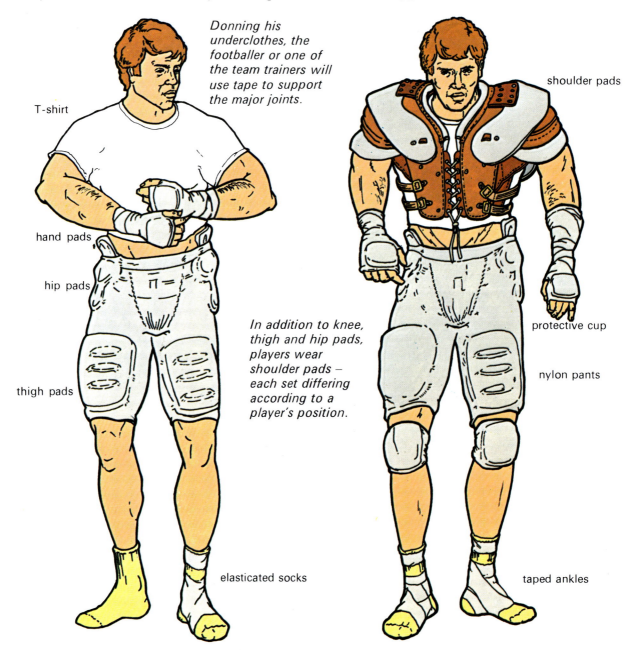

Donning his underclothes, the footballer or one of the team trainers will use tape to support the major joints.

T-shirt

hand pads

hip pads

thigh pads

In addition to knee, thigh and hip pads, players wear shoulder pads – each set differing according to a player's position.

elasticated socks

shoulder pads

protective cup

nylon pants

taped ankles

STAGE TWO

Weighing in at 6 lb (2.7 kg), the shoulder pads are the heaviest item of a player's equipment. Made of tough, modern materials such as vinyl, nylon and foam rubber, the size of the pads vary according to a player's position. Wrist and elbow pads may also go on at this stage, as well as biceps pads and shin guards.

STAGE THREE

Next come the player's uniform – his

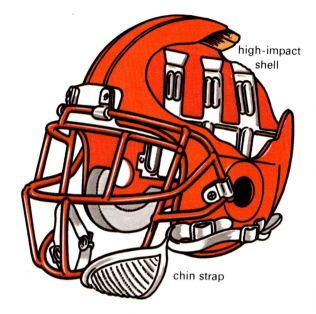

high-impact shell

chin strap

The modern helmet's padding and liquid-filled cells are shaped through use to provide each player with a custom fit.

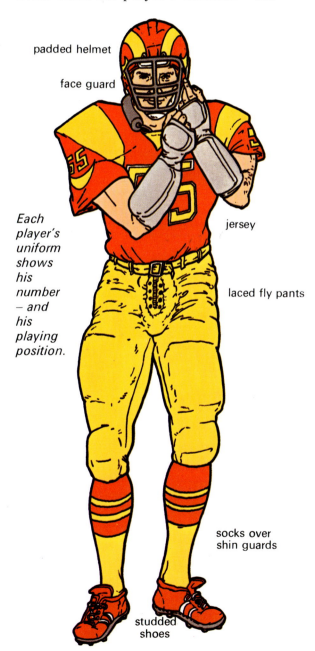

padded helmet

face guard

Each player's uniform shows his number – and his playing position.

jersey

laced fly pants

socks over shin guards

studded shoes

shirt, socks and pants. The studs on the undersides of his playing shoes will reflect the type of surface he is about to play on – seven or eight rubberized studs for grass, many more, shorter studs for artificial surfaces. Finally, a player will pull on his helmet, which is a highly sophisticated item featuring special padding and liquid-filled cells to cushion the impact of blows to the head. Attached to the helmet is a face cage to prevent serious injuries.

In addition to their protective equipment, players try to lessen the severity of possible injuries by keeping as fit as possible. Before the American National Football League (NFL) season begins, the players of each club undergo a five-week fitness and skills programme called training camp, well away from the distractions of wives, girlfriends and nightclubs. There they develop their strength and speed – with devastating results.

HEAD ON

Players today are fitter, stronger and better protected than ever before. Yet when two 270 lb (122.5 kg) supermen collide at top speed, something has to give.

MEET THE PLAYERS

Unlike games such as soccer where all team members become attackers when in possession of the ball and defenders when they're not, an American football team is divided into three units – the offense, the defense and the special teams unit. These units take each other's places on the gridiron according to the state of the game since there is no limit to the number of substitutes used. The offense will take the field when handed possession of the ball, the defense when the opposing team has the ball, and the special teams unit comes on in certain situations such as kick-offs, punts and extra point attempts.

THE OFFENSE

The basic offense is made up of five linemen, three receivers, two running-backs and a quarterback, but coaches may make changes to this format as the game progresses. Seven players must line up on the line of scrimmage before each play.

Offensive linemen Two guards, two tackles and a center man the interior offensive line. Their main task is to blast open holes in the defense for the running-backs to run through, and to protect the quarterback as he is about to pass. The center passes or "snaps" the ball to the quarterback at the beginning of the play. The interior linemen may not receive a pass or a hand-off.

Quarterback He is the leader of the offense. After receiving the snap from the centre, he may either hand the ball to a runningback, pass it downfield to a receiver or run with it himself.

Runningbacks These are the ball-carriers. Runningbacks come in two forms – the fullback, a big and powerful runner, and the halfback who is often a little quicker, more agile and sometimes throws passes. Both may receive passes.

Wide receivers These players are the prime targets of the quarterback's pass downfield and are usually split several

Quarterback: A strong and accurate passer of the ball, the quarterback is also the leader of the offense

Fullback: The bigger of the two running backs, the fullback is a powerful runner who must also be able to block effectivley for his backfield partner, the halfback

THE PLAYERS AND THEIR POSITIONS

Halfback: The smaller, more agile halfback may also be used to make passes

yards from the rest of the offense.

Tight end The tight end joins the interior linemen on the line of scrimmage but may also receive passes. He can line up either to the left or to the right of the other linemen and the side he joins is called the strong side because of the extra help he brings.

THE DEFENSE

The players making up the defense can line up on or off the line as they wish.

Defensive end There are two defensive ends which take opposite sides of the defensive formation at the line of scrimmage. Their main responsibility is to tackle the quarterback before he passes

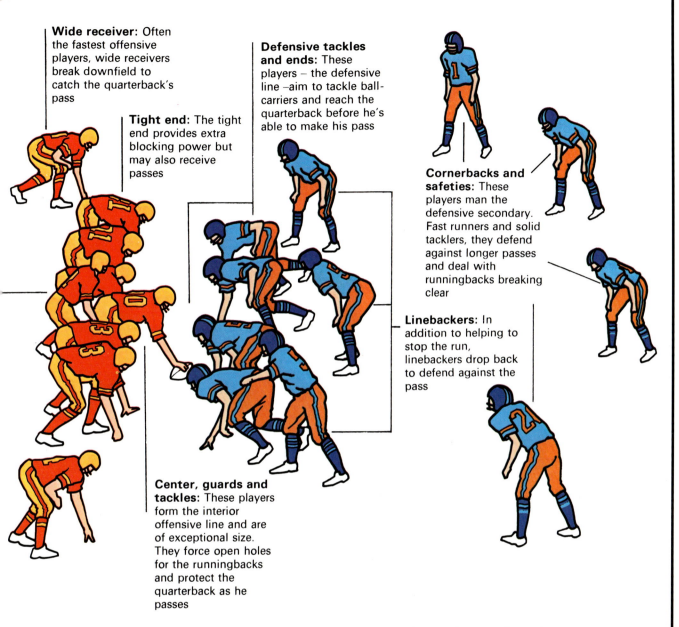

Wide receiver: Often the fastest offensive players, wide receivers break downfield to catch the quarterback's pass

Tight end: The tight end provides extra blocking power but may also receive passes

Defensive tackles and ends: These players – the defensive line –aim to tackle ball-carriers and reach the quarterback before he's able to make his pass

Cornerbacks and safeties: These players man the defensive secondary. Fast runners and solid tacklers, they defend against longer passes and deal with runningbacks breaking clear

Linebackers: In addition to helping to stop the run, linebackers drop back to defend against the pass

Center, guards and tackles: These players form the interior offensive line and are of exceptional size. They force open holes for the runningbacks and protect the quarterback as he passes

the ball, but also to stop the ball-carriers (runningbacks).

Defensive tackle A 4–3 defensive formation (four defenders on the line of scrimmage, and three linebackers) will have two defensive tackles, a 3–4 formation (three men on the line of scrimmage and four linebackers) will have just one. These players share the same duties as the defensive ends and, with them, form the defensive line.

Linebackers Linebackers play just off the line of scrimmage, tackling ball-carriers, breaking through the defensive line and covering against the pass.

Cornerbacks The left and right cornerbacks play further away from the line of scrimmage in an area of the field called the defensive backfield or secondary. They cover wide receivers on pass plays.

Safeties The two safeties play in the secondary, the strong safety on the tight end's side, the free safety wherever he wishes. Pass coverage is their main role but they may also have to stop ball-carriers. Together with the cornerbacks, they make up the defensive backs.

THE OFFENSE

To "rookie" American football fans, or those new to the game, an offensive play looks like a very disorganized affair which always seems to end up in a 22-body pile-up. There are plenty of collisions, certainly, but things are anything but disorganized.

THE HUDDLE

In fact, the play that the offense uses to move the ball downfield is decided beforehand by coaches on the sideline and relayed out to the quarterback. He then passes details of the play to the rest of the offence in the *huddle* where the players come together in a group some 10 yards (9.1 m) behind the ball.

THE SNAP

The play called may be either a pass or a run (the coaches may decide to punt, but that's a job for special teams, see page 18) but both use the same method to bring the ball into play – the *snap*. Here, on the command word the center passes the ball through his legs to the quarterback.

The ball is now in the quarterback's hands, and huge defenders are thundering towards him. How does he move the ball downfield?

RUSHING

On a running play (which is known as rushing), the quarterback will hand or pitch the ball out to one of his running-

hand-off

pitchout

blocking

The hand-off: *On a running play, the quarterback will hand the ball after the snap to one of his runningbacks.*

The pitchout: *To gain extra speed and width on the play, a quarterback may instead pitch the ball out to a runningback.*

Blocking: *The ball-carrier relies on good blocking from his team-mates to clear him a path downfield.*

backs. They may run outside (between the end of the offensive line and the sideline), inside (between the two offensive tackles) or up the middle (through the centre position), but whichever route the play demands they take, they won't get very far without good blocking from their team-mates. Here, the offensive players try to create gaps in the offensive line for the runningbacks to rush through by knocking defenders out of the way.

Blocking is pre-planned. Each offensive player receives a blocking assignment in the form of a defender who must be stopped from reaching the ball-carrier. These blocking patterns vary according to the running play called and the offensive formation being used.

THE SWEEP

A popular running play that shows the importance of good blocking is the sweep where, after receiving the ball from the quarterback – the "hand-off" – the runningback runs outside his offensive line and heads upfield. To be able to do so, he needs the help of his guards who, on the snap, pull back from their positions, run behind the line of scrimmage in the direction of the play and block any defenders moving towards him. This is pulling.

A ball-carrier must be careful not to fumble the ball, that is to drop it as he is running or when he is tackled by a defender. A fumble may be recovered by the defence and advanced downfield where the recovering team's offense will then take possession.

The typical offensive play-book will feature many different types of running play, each using different players to execute them and selecting different points of attack. A reverse, for example, is where the quarterback hands-off to a runningback going in one direction, and he then hands-off to a runningback going in the other. In a draw play, the quarterback pretends he is about to pass the ball, making defenders cross the line of scrimmage, and then hands-off to a runningback who heads for a gap created by the rushing defenders.

Carrying out these comparatively simple plays effectively takes hours of practice. The razzle-dazzle plays – the one-off spectaculars – can take weeks.

The sweep: *The two guards in the middle of the diagram are "pulling" – moving in the direction of the play to block defenders trying to tackle the ball-carrier.*

PASSING

The key to an effective passing game is again good blocking. The quarterback must be given enough time to get the ball away before the defenders break through. If he is tackled before he can release his pass to his receivers downfield, he is said to have been sacked – a painful experience in the National Football League!

The offensive linemen use different techniques when blocking passes. Instead of firing out into the defensive line as on a running play, the linemen take a few steps back off the line, fending off rushing defenders as they go. Runningbacks may also be used on pass protection duty, blocking any defenders who are threatening to break through.

The quarterback drops back into the area surrounded by his offensive wall.

Above: *The success of a pass depends on split-second timing, pin-point accuracy and good co-ordination between quarterback and receiver.*

This area is known as the pocket. From there he decides whether his receiver is in a good position to receive his pass. Normally, he will only pass the ball if his receiver has got open – that is if the receiver is clear of the defensive backs for a few moments. But he may be forced into a hurried, inaccurate pass by on-coming rushers. Such passes are liable to be intercepted by linebackers and defensive backs since these players have the same right to the ball as the receiver, but may not hinder him in making the catch beyond 5 yards (4.6 m) of the line of scrimmage.

As the ball is snapped, the receiver (who may also be a runningback or a tight end) begins a very carefully mapped-out route downfield according to the play called. By running to strict patterns, the

Left: *The snap. The center brings the ball into play by snapping it through his legs to the quarterback.*

BASIC FORMATION

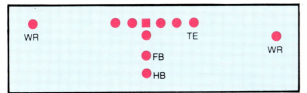

I-Formation: *A strong running formation, both runningbacks line up behind the quarterback.*

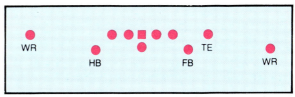

Spread: *This formation allows five receivers to break downfield quickly on passing plays.*

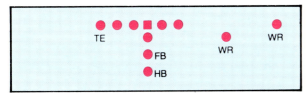

Pro-set: *With the runningbacks split either side of the quarterback, the pro-set can be used for both pass and run.*

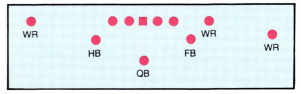

Shotgun: *A pure passing formation, the quarterback takes the snap some six yard deep to give himself extra time to pass.*

receivers are trying to help the quarterback, who must know exactly when to release his pass.

THE SHORT PASSING GAME

The most exciting of all passing plays is the "bomb", a very high pass to a receiver downfield, who is often in or near the endzone. But short passes can be very effective, too, particularly when combined with a little cunning and deception. In a screen pass, for example, the offensive linemen deliberately let defenders through to the quarterback after blocking poorly on the line, but regroup in front of a tight end or wide receiver waiting off to the side. At just the right moment, the quarterback tosses the ball over the heads of charging defenders to the receiver, who then has a screen of blockers to protect him on his run downfield.

The play-action pass is another useful short passing tool. Here, the offensive linemen prepare to block for a running play while the quarterback fakes a hand-off to the runningback, who continues on through the line. If the linebackers are fooled into defending the run and lured towards the line of scrimmage to plug the gaps, a short pass to another runningback running into the area they have just left

can gain valuable yardage.

Carrying out a pass, timing and co-ordination are very important to all offensive plays. And knowing when to use which pass can also mean the difference between winning and losing. On third and long (where the offense is on its third down chance but still has a long way to go to win another first down), for example, the defense will be expecting a pass since they generally produce more yardage. The defense will be rushing hard – the ideal time to run the draw play.

On a play-action pass play, the quarterback first deceives the defense by faking a hand-off to a runningback.

THE DEFENSE

Many great defensive players claim that they eat quarterbacks for breakfast and they enjoy the fearsome reputation that has grown up around them. But it would be wrong to think of the men on defense as undisciplined bullies. Like their offensive colleagues, they use skill, strategy and deception to perform their roles – it just hurts more when they tackle you!

DEFENSIVE FORMATIONS

The 4-3 The two major defensive formations in the game today are the 4-3 and the 3-4, though others may be used for certain situations. The 4-3 features four linemen on the line of scrimmage and three linebackers a yard (1 m) or more behind. This formation is not used quite as often as the 3-4 but is, nevertheless, a strong pass-rushing formation because of the four down linemen, who are also in a good position to plug the gaps on running plays quickly. The three linebackers have a lot of ground to cover, though, and the 4-3 sometimes struggles against the short, flat pass.

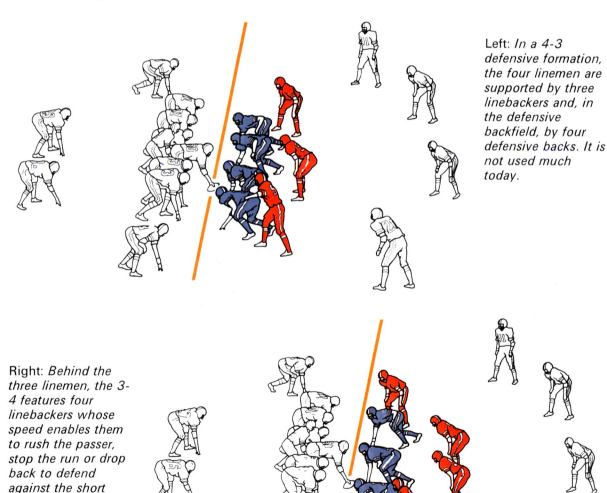

Left: *In a 4-3 defensive formation, the four linemen are supported by three linebackers and, in the defensive backfield, by four defensive backs. It is not used much today.*

Right: *Behind the three linemen, the 3-4 features four linebackers whose speed enables them to rush the passer, stop the run or drop back to defend against the short pass.*

The 3-4 Here, two defensive ends and a nose tackle line up on the line of scrimmage, the ends over, or to one side of the offensive tackles, and the nose directly over the centre. All four linebackers are still able to rush the passer from their deep positions as well as dropping back to provide extra pass protection. On running plays, the inside linebackers are in a good position to tackle runners breaking through the middle of the line, while the quicker outside linebackers will force ball-carriers running wide to move in towards their stronger, less mobile colleagues.

Nickels and dimes – passing defenses In both the 4-3 and 3-4, the use of four defensive backs – the two cornerbacks and the two safeties – is the same. When it is clear that the offense has no option but to pass – when trailing by 12 points late in the game, for example – the defense will strengthen its protection against the pass by bringing in extra defensive backs at the expense of the linebackers. One extra defensive back makes it a nickel defense, two extra backs makes it a dime defense.

The flex – a running defense A variation of the 4-3 is the flex, a version which can oppose a strong running game. Any two of the four linemen line up a few yards off the line of scrimmage, while the two others line up as usual and the linebackers fill up the holes.

Instead of strengthening the pass rush, the 'flex' aims to stop the run, because the two linemen just off the line are not used as pass rushers. They read the play first, which makes it easier for them to react to the run.

Above: *On some passing plays, particularly dangerous receivers may draw double coverage where they are marked by two defenders. This may create an opportunity for another receiver elsewhere.*

Below: *The flex is a 4-3 defense designed to stop running plays. Two linemen take their positions just off the line of scrimmage.*

Right: *Close to their own goal-line, defenses substitute defensive backs for bigger linemen, who then line up low opposite the gaps in the offensive line to undermine the blocking of their opponents.*

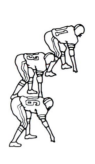

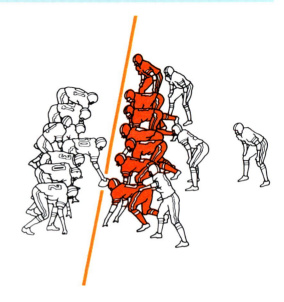

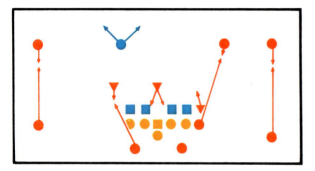

Above: *A defense playing man-to-man coverage will use a defensive back or linebacker to shadow each potential receiver.*

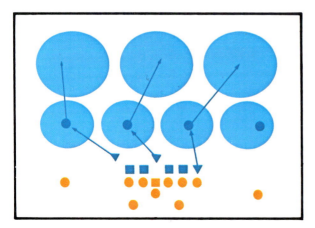

Above: *More common nowadays are zone coverages where pass defenders drop back into certain areas of the field to cover receivers.*

To play the game effectively, defenders must be able to spot the type of play the offense is running as soon as possible. By watching certain players and areas of the field (their *keys*), the defender tries to work out, as the ball is snapped, how the play will unfold. He then reacts according to how he thinks the game will develop – which may not be accurate since the offense might give false clues.

The strong side linebacker in the 4-3, for example, will first key on the tight end. If he stays around the line of scrimmage to block, the linebacker will get ready for a running play. If the tight end heads off on a pattern, the linebacker will prepare to cover him for the pass. His second priority is the action of the guards who may be pulling behind the line of scrimmage. If they are, the linebacker moves in to take one of them out or break up the play by tackling the ball-carrier. If not, the linebacker waits for the next runningback to enter his area.

ZONE DEFENSE

In defending against the pass, many defenses use zone defenses where the pass defenders – the linebackers and the defensive backs – are responsible for cover-

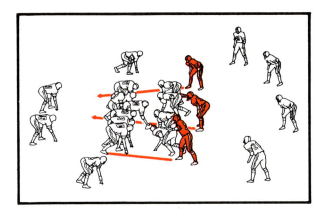

Above: *Dogs and blitzes are both surprise pass-rushing plays. A dog uses one or more linebackers to reach the quarterback.*

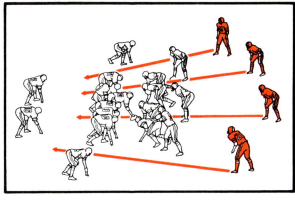

Above: *The aim of a blitz is also to reach the quarterback before he passes. This time, defensive backs are used.*

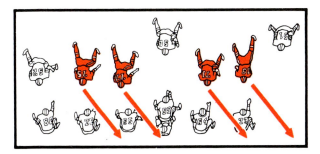

Above: *Defensive linemen using a slant try to unsettle the offense by each attacking to one side instead of straight ahead.*

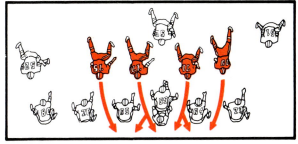

Above: *The aim of a pinch is to upset the offensive blocking scheme by trapping one or more offensive linemen.*

ing certain sectors of the field. The defensive players move into the middle of these zones on the snap but do not react to receivers entering their zone until the ball has been thrown. Once the ball is in the air, they rush towards the receiver.

If a receiver leaves a short zone for a deeper one, the defender in the new zone has to cover him. In this way, two slower defensive backs are able to deal with a lightning-fast receiver who, in the other system of man-to-man coverage, would out-run them and lose them for long enough to receive a pass.

DEFENSIVE MOVES

Modern defenses do not just sit back and wait for the offensive play to unfold. Instead, they will use tactics of their own to surprise, unsettle and put off the men trying to put touchdowns past them.
Dogging and blitzing Rushing the passer from deeper positions can catch the offense unawares. In a dog, one or more linebackers attack the passer, timing their run so that they cross the line of scrimmage just as the ball is snapped. A blitz is another surprise pass rush, this time involving a defensive back.

Stacks, pinches and slants Slants and pinches are tricks performed by defensive linemen. In a slant, all linemen attack the offensive line from either the right or the left. This makes the defence more effective because the linemen know exactly what they are going to do as soon as they get into position.

A *pinch* is where the defensive linemen rush on one or more offensive linemen, hemming them in so tightly that they are unable to block properly. If a linebacker lines up directly behind a lineman in a stack formation, it can be very difficult for the offence to judge his direction of attack.

SPECIAL TEAMS

The special teamers on the roster are the players who deal with the team's kicking and kick-returning responsibilities. They do not always get the praise they deserve. But in a close game, good special teams play can mean the difference between winning and losing.

KICK-OFFS

Kick-offs are taken from a tee placed on the 35 yard (32 m) line to start each half and after a team has scored, the scoring team receiving the kick-off. The best kick-offs are high and deep so that the kicking

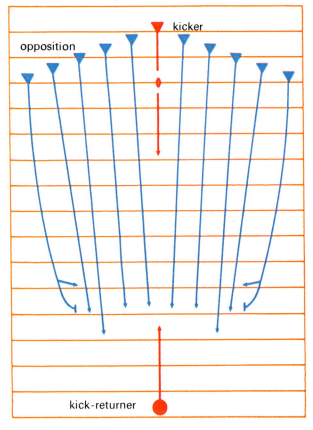

The kick-off coverage team must quickly close down the kick-off returner.

Left: *On fieldgoal and PAT kicks, the holder takes a long snap from the center and sets the ball up* (left) *for the kicker* (below), *whose kick must clear on-rushing defenders.*

team has enough time to get downfield to cover the kick, and the kick-returner must start his run upfield from the shadow of his own posts. The kicking team stays in formation as it runs downfield to cover the kick, in order to close off all routes to the kick-returner.

Sometimes, the kick-off team will use an on-side kick, usually if behind in points and needing to recover possession. Here, the kicker will kick the ball only a short distance downfield. Since the ball becomes anyone's after travelling more than 10 yards (9.1 m), the aim of the kicking team is to grab possession again before the receiving team can react.

The first group of blockers on a kick-

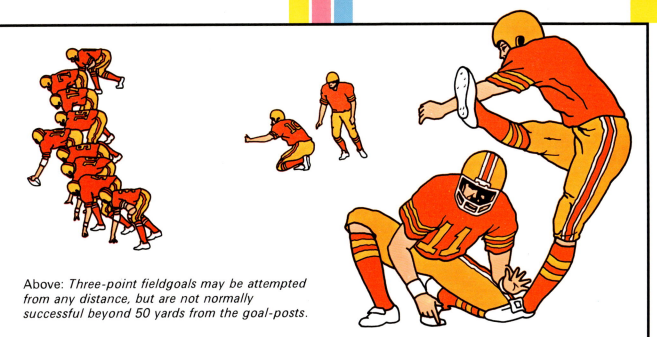

Above: *Three-point fieldgoals may be attempted from any distance, but are not normally successful beyond 50 yards from the goal-posts.*

return unit try to stop this ploy. The second group forms a wedge around the ball-carrier to clear a path for him up-field. The fact that there are 11 men out to tackle him before he gets a few yards upfield, let alone return the ball for a touchdown, means the kick-returner must be a brave man – or a lunatic!

FIELDGOALS AND PATS

On fieldgoal and PAT (point after touch-down) attempts, the center snaps the ball

Right: *A punter aims to kick as far and high as possible, so his team-mates have time to close down the punt returner.*

some 7 yards (6.4 m) or so back to the holder, who places the ball in an upright position for the kicker. In an attempt to block the kick, the opposing team will staff its line with its tallest players and try to penetrate the kicker's own protective wall.

PUNTS

The punter and his special teams col-leagues are normally called for on fourth down when the offense is still well short of another first down. By punting, the offense loses possession of the ball but makes its opponents begin their drive deeper inside their own half. This time, the center has to snap the ball 12–15 yards (10.9–13.7 m) to the punter who kicks the ball from his own hands.

Again, height and distance are import-ant on a punt. The punt-receiving team will decide to make either a big effort to block the punt, or concentrate on return-ing it as far upfield as possible.

If it tries to block the punt, there will be a fierce rush of opposing players from all sides. If the decision is to go for a good return, its linemen will each pick an opponent and prevent him from blocking the punt-returner's path upfield. The route the punt-returner takes is usually decided before the play begins.

STRATEGY AND COMMUNICATION

PLAY-CALLING

The tactical supremo of an American football team is the head coach. He has with him on the sidelines a number of coaching assistants, including the team's offensive and defensive co-ordinators. In addition, he is linked via a radio head-set to coaching staff seated in the press-box high in the stands, who have a much better view of what is happening in the middle of the field.

Before making his final decision as to which play shall be run, the head coach will also bear in mind his game-plan, a carefully prepared outline for the game in hand, which includes a list of plays specially designed to take advantage of his opponents' weaknesses.

RELAYING THE MESSAGE

Once the coach has made up his mind, the decision will be sent out to the quar-

huddle   messenger   head-coach   owner's booth

The coaches watching from the press-box, the head coach, his assistants and the players are all in constant communication. The head coach (left) talks to his colleagues in the press-box via a head-set and the message is relayed onto the field by the players themselves or via hand-signals.

The offense may try to confuse the defense by putting a man in motion to change its formation. Here, one player is allowed to move parallel to, or backward from the line of scrimmage before the play begins, cutting upfield on the snap to become a lead blocker or receiver.

Below right: The hole numbering system is a sort of shorthand in playcalling. Each hole beside the interior linemen is given a number; odd numbers to the left, even to the right. The spaces the runningbacks stand in are also numbered.

terback via hand-signals made by an assistant, or by an offensive player coming on to take another's place.

The quarterback briefs his team-mates on the play to be run using a verbal shorthand in the huddle. He might say:

'Power-I Right (The offensive formation and the side the tight end takes),

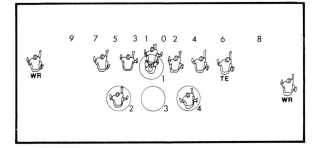

| 9 | 7 | 5 | 3 | 1 | 0 | 2 | 4 | 6 | 8 |

43 THE NUMBER OF THE PLAY

The popularity of the 43 has declined somewhat since the 1970s but virtually every team still uses it in certain game situations. To make communication in the huddle quicker and clearer, running plays are numbered according to the runningback used and the hole he runs through. In the Power-1, for example, the Number Four back heads for the Number Three hole, hence the '43' called in the huddle. Each team uses its own numbering sequence.

calling an audible to his team-mates at the line of scrimmage. Here, he will call out the "live" colour agreed for that game and the number of the new play. His team-mates, once alerted by the live colour call and having memorized the action of each play and its number, will perform their roles according to the new play.

THE SNAP COUNT

The snap count tells the offense when the ball is going to be snapped. At the line of scrimmage, the quarterback makes a series of calls which sound like "hike, hike, hike!". "On Two" means that the ball will be snapped on the second "hike". Armed with this information, the offense has a fraction of a second's advantage over the defense.

43 (The number of the play), On Two (The *snap count*), Break!'

If, on seeing how the defense is lining up, the quarterback feels the play called will not work, he will change the play by

THE OFFICIALS

Seven men are needed to officiate at an American football game. Sometimes referred to as zebras because of their black and white striped uniforms, the officials face a huge task in making sure the NFL rules are followed. One veteran NFL referee likened his duties to "trying to maintain order during a legalized brawl involving 80 toughs with a little whistle, a hanky and a ton of prayer".

In fact, bad behaviour is extremely rare and while coaches rant and rave on the sidelines (and the Chicago Bears' coach Mike Ditka might throw his clipboard around), they accept that the referee's decision is final.

The hanky referred to is a square of yellow cloth called a flag which each member of the officiating team carries in his pocket and throws to the ground when he sees an infringement, or breaking of

the rules. The referee's decision is relayed to the fans in the stands via a microphone attached to his shirt and a series of hand-signals.

The referee heads the officiating team and makes the final decision on what the rules mean. He has the power to send any player off the field and usually lines up about 10 yards (9.1 m) behind the line of scrimmage where he has a good view of the quarterback and the area where fumbles often occur. (Teams are penalized by having the ball moved back towards their own goal-line.)

The umpire stands 4–5 yards (3.7–4.6 m) behind the linebackers, checking that no interior offensive lineman moves after going into his three-point

Below: *The game officials use hand signals and a microphone link-up to convey their decisions to the fans.*

time out   touchdown, fieldgoal   personal foul   illegal use of hands, arms or body   illegal contact   delay

offside or encroaching   holding   illegal motion   first down   interference with forward pass or fair catch   penalty refused, incomplete pass, play over, or missed fieldgoal

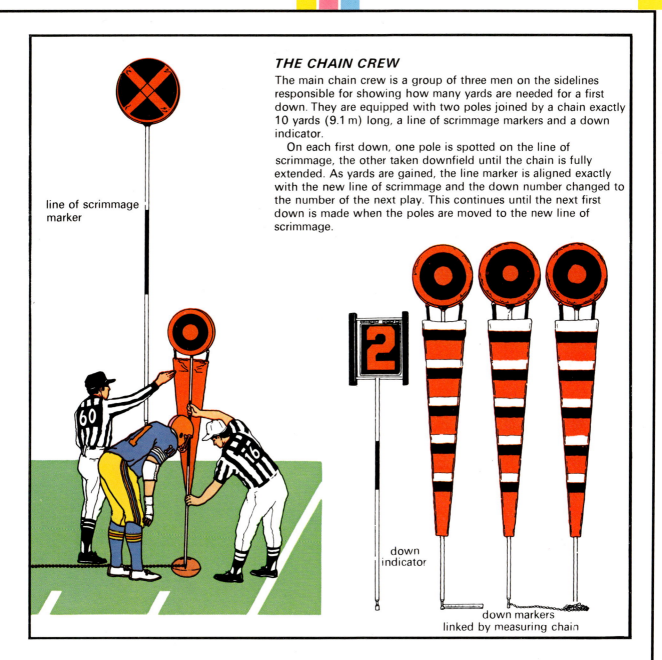

THE CHAIN CREW

The main chain crew is a group of three men on the sidelines responsible for showing how many yards are needed for a first down. They are equipped with two poles joined by a chain exactly 10 yards (9.1 m) long, a line of scrimmage markers and a down indicator.

On each first down, one pole is spotted on the line of scrimmage, the other taken downfield until the chain is fully extended. As yards are gained, the line marker is aligned exactly with the new line of scrimmage and the down number changed to the number of the next play. This continues until the next first down is made when the poles are moved to the new line of scrimmage.

line of scrimmage marker

down indicator

down markers linked by measuring chain

stance and that the offensive blocking is legal. The head linesman checks that no player crosses the line of scrimmage before the snap and watches over the chain crew on the sideline. The line judge stands with one foot on either side of the scrimmage line on the side opposite the head linesman's, and checks on the path of the wide receivers on his side and the legality of passes.

The back judge patrols the same side of the field as the line judge but from a position 15–17 yards (13.7–15.5 m) off the line of scrimmage. From there, he keeps an eye on the tight end and nearest back as well as assuming responsibility for pass interference, holding and illegal use of hand calls. The field judge stands some 25 yards (22.9 m) downfield. One of his duties is to time the 30-second interval from the end of the last play to the beginning of a new one, since the offense is penalized if the ball is not brought into play within this period. The side judge has many duties, overlapping those of other officials.

THE NATIONAL FOOTBALL LEAGUE

Anyone drawing up a list of the world's greatest sporting competitions would have to place the National Football League (NFL) up there with the best of them. The 28-team extravaganza has all the right ingredients – glamour, excitement and professionalism – to produce a winter sports spectacle rivalling any other.

The NFL's clubs are divided into two conferences of 14 – the American Football Conference (AFC) and the National Football Conference (NFC). In each conference, there are three divisions: AFC East, AFC Central and AFC West; and NFC East, NFC Central and NFC West.

The clubs do battle over a 16-game regular season to earn a place in the play-offs, the final rounds of the competition. The two conference winners then go forward to contest the Super Bowl, a game staged at a different location each year, to find American football's world champion.

The NFL year starts in mid-August with four pre-season games where the teams are able to experiment with different tactics and new players before deciding on their final 45-man roster. Then, round about the middle of September, they begin their regular season schedule which includes two games played at home and away against each of the rivals in its division. In addition, teams will play opponents from other divisions and conferences according to a special formula.

The teams with the best overall records in each of the six divisions then go forward to the play-offs, together with the two teams from each conference with the next best records who qualify as 'wild cards'. The two wild cards in each conference meet and the winner progresses to the divisional play-offs. The two clubs in each conference emerging from those battles face each other in the conference championships. The two winners of the

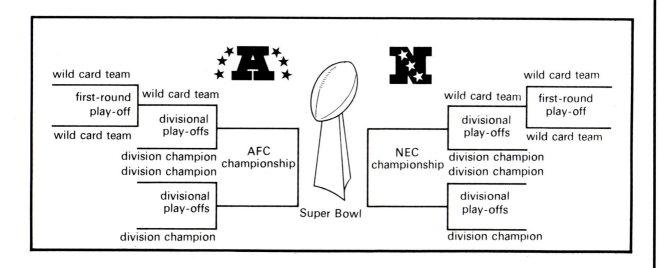

wild card team

first-round play-off

wild card team

wild card team

divisional play-offs

AFC championship

division champion
division champion

divisional play-offs

division champion

Super Bowl

wild card team

NEC championship

divisional play-offs

division champion
division champion

divisional play-offs

division champion

wild card team

first-round play-off

wild card team

conference championships then advance to the Super Bowl where the Vince Lombardi Trophy and a set of winners' rings are at stake.

The first Super Bowl was played in January 1967 between the Green Bay Packers of the National Football League and the Kansas City Chiefs of the American Football League, in the days when two leagues existed in football. Vince Lombardi, one of the greatest coaches the game has ever seen, led the Packers to a 35–10 victory, and, in Super Bowl II a year later, to a 33–14 win over the Oakland Raiders. The two leagues merged in 1970 to form the new National Football League.

The most successful of all Super Bowl teams has been the Pittsburgh Steelers who carried off four Super Bowl titles during the 1970s.

Below: *A tense moment between the Los Angeles Rams and the Atlanta Falcons.*

KEY TO HELMETS OPPOSITE

NATIONAL FOOTBALL CONFERENCE (NFC)

 1 Chicago Bears
 2 Green Bay Packers
 3 Minnesota Vikings
 4 San Francisco 49ers
 5 St Louis Cardinals
 6 Detroit Lions
 7 Atlanta Falcons
 8 New York Giants
 9 New Orleans Saints
10 Dallas Cowboys
11 Washington Redskins
12 Philadelphia Eagles
13 Tampa Bay Buccaneers
14 Los Angeles Rams

AMERICAN FOOTBALL CONFERENCE (AFC)

15 San Diego Chargers
16 Miami Dolphins
17 Buffalo Bills
18 New England Patriots
19 Pittsburgh Steelers
20 New York Jets
21 Cleveland Browns
22 Cincinnati Bengals
23 Los Angeles Raiders
24 Indianapolis Colts
25 Denver Broncos
26 Kansas City Chiefs
27 Seattle Seahawks
28 Houston Oilers

MASTERING THE BASICS

The young gridiron player, in common with budding stars in other sports, has a series of first-stage techniques to learn if he is to play the game well. To improve his understanding of the game, a young player should learn the basics of as many positions as possible before commiting himself to the same role as his idol.

BLOCKING

There are different types of block, all using slightly different techniques but the basic shoulder block is the most important one to know. When throwing the shoulder block, remember to *fire straight out* at your opponents, keeping your head up.

- Make the first contact with your shoulder but follow it up by pushing your forearm firmly up into your opponent's chest and then stay in contact with him.
- Always put your head and body between your opponent and the ball-carrier.
- Keep your feet spread wide so that you have a good solid base from which to continue driving into your man, even after the first hit has been made.
- Still staying in contact with him and driving your feet forwards, try to turn your back to the hole you are trying to create by swinging your hips round after making that first hit.

TACKLING

The most important quality for any tackler is a determination to bring the ball-carrier down. Tackles don't have to look good but that star runningback must be stopped.

To make an effective tackle, try to give yourself time to get in a good, low hitting position as the runner approaches you.

Keep your eyes on his stomach so as not to be foiled by any sudden shoulder or head movements, and hit him there hard with your shoulder. Then close your arms around him, making sure you grab something to hold on to, such as his shirt. It's important to keep your legs driving to kill his momentum, which could give him an extra yard for the first down.

Far left: *When blocking, make contact first with your shoulder, keeping your head between the opponent and the ball-carrier. Keep your head up, push up hard with your forearm and keep your feet driving.*

Left: *When tackling, keep low as you approach the ball-carrier* (top), *hit hard with your shoulder,* (centre) *and wrap him up with your arms, keeping your feet driving. You should aim to stop him cold.*

Above: *Good runningbacks don't have to look at the ball as it's handed off to them. Simply make a pocket with your arms* (left) *and let the quarterback do the rest* (right).

THE HAND-OFF

On a running play, the quarterback will take the snap, pivot and hand-off to the runningback. If you are the running back, remember that it's the quarterback's job to give you the ball, not yours to take it from him.

As you approach the point where the quarterback will give you the ball, make a pocket with your arms by raising your arm nearest the quarterback horizontally and keeping the other level with your stomach. Do not make life difficult for the quarterback by snatching for the ball – just let him put it there gently.

CONTROLLING THE BALL

THE GRIP

The most important thing when learning to throw the ball is to get a proper grip. It may be wise to practise your passing on junior-sized footballs first, to develop the right passing action before moving up to the full-sized senior ball.

First of all, spread your fingers as far as you can down the laces of the ball without straining them too much. The little finger should be clasped hard on to the laces, the thumb curled around the middle of the ball, and the index finger placed across the ball's seam. This grip will give you the control you need.

THROWING

Passes are thrown by swiftly rotating the whole of your upper body and your hips, not merely by flicking the wrist, however easily professional players are able to do so.

If you are a right-handed passer, begin the passing action by rotating your body until your left side is lined up with the target. Pull your left shoulder up under your chin in preparation for the pass. Move your front forward in the direction of your receiver and, holding your left elbow high, use it to quickly pull round

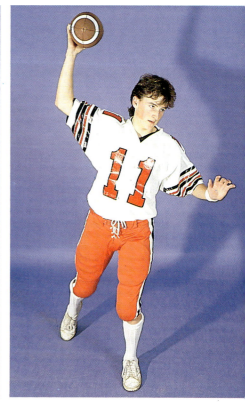

your left arm, shoulders and throwing arm, whipping round your hips at the same time.

This movement transfers your body weight from your right to your left side. As this rotation of the upper body and hips gathers momentum, lift your right arm up high and forwards and release the ball at the highest point your arm reaches as the twisting of the body pulls it through. Pull down with your left arm and shoulder as you swing round, continuing the rotation as you follow through.

RECEIVING

The best receivers, it has been said, have made themselves the best through practice rather than having been born with a wealth of natural talent.

The first thing to remember when making the catch is to concentrate. Watch the ball as it drops, and don't take your eyes off it until it lands in your hands. Secondly, it is important to relax your hands rather than tense them up when waiting for the catch. Thirdly, remember to catch the ball with your fingers rather than with your palms.

When making a catch with your arms outstretched, hold the fingers of one hand out in front of the path of the ball. Use your other hand to make a net underneath. Bring your thumbs together one hand on top of another when catching a ball above your head.

If the ball arrives at waist height, point your fingers towards the ground, opening your palms to the ball. If the pass is low, put your little fingers together and form a net underneath the ball, keeping your body behind it to shield it from defenders who might take advantage of a mishandled ball.

GLOSSARY

Alley-oop A high pass made by the quarterback over the heads of pass defenders in the hope that his receiver can skirt the defensive coverage and get to the ball first.

Bootleg A piece of deception by the quarterback where he fakes a hand-off to a runningback before concealing the ball beside his hip and rolling out to one side in a bid to gain yards himself.

defence down the middle.

Holding The illegal use of hands to grab on to an opponent, most commonly associated with players on the offensive line. Results in a 10-yard (9.1 m) penalty.

In-bounds The area bounded by the sidelines and goal-lines. When receiving, receivers must have both feet on the ground and be in-bounds for the pass to be ruled complete.

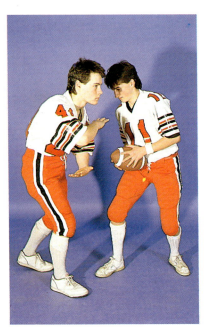  

Clipping An illegal block from behind, usually made by throwing the body across the back of an opponent's legs. Clipping is permissible within 3 yards (2.7 m) of the line of scrimmage, but will result in a 15-yard (13.7 m) penalty anywhere else.

Coughing-up A fumble of the ball resulting in a loss of possession.

Fair catch A type of punt reception where the player on the receiving team making the catch raises his arm while the ball is still in the air. This signal means that he does not intend to run with the ball after it has been caught, and allows him to make the catch unhindered.

Goodnight, Irene A long touchdown pass or run which completely splits a

Above: *For a bootleg to work, the faked hand-off must look as realistic as possible. The quarterback slips the ball down beside his hip and rolls out, often picking up a blocker before attempting to sprint into the end zone.*

Intentional grounding The action of a quarterback who deliberately throws the ball away to avoid being tackled for a loss of yards. Results in a 10-yard (9.1 m) penalty and a loss of down.

Late-hit A player making contact with an opponent after the ball has been passed. Results in a 15-yard (13.7 m) penalty.

Overshift The movement of defensive linemen one full position to the strong side of a formation at the line of scrimmage. While interior offensive linemen may not move before the snap after taking a three-point stance, defensive players may move as they please.

Pigskin The football, which, in fact, is not made of pigskin but of ordinary leather.

Turnover The transfer of possession following a fumble recovery, pass interception or the blocking and recovering of a punt or fieldgoal.

Left: Clipping may not be used to block opponents, except within three yards each side of the line of scrimmage. During kick-offs, no clipping is allowed at all.

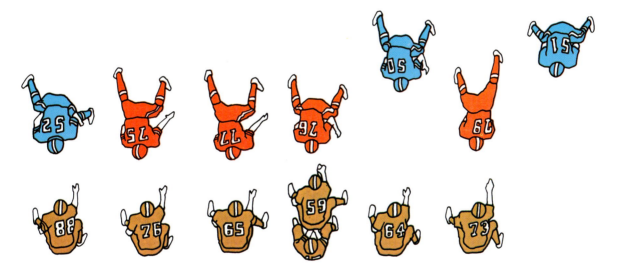

Above: Overshifts (and undershifts to the weak side) are used by the defense to try to upset the offense at what it thinks is the most likely angle of attack.

Below: An NFL football weighs between 395 and 425 g (14–15 oz).

Muff An unsuccessful attempt by a player to gain possession of a loose ball.

Neutral zone An imaginary area the width of a ball's length that separates the two teams at the line of scrimmage. No player may enter this area until the ball is snapped.

Index

Published in 1988 by
The Hamlyn Publishing Group Limited
a division of Paul Hamlyn Publishing
Michelin House, 81 Fulham Road, London SW3 6RB

Copyright © The Hamlyn Publishing Group Limited 1988

ISBN 0 600 55738 3

Printed and bound in Italy
Front jacket illustration: All-Sport, Stuart Brendan
Illustrations: Stuart Brendan
Photographic acknowledgments: Ian Christy, All-Sport
Design: Bob Burroughs
General editors: Gillian Denton, Lynne Williams

The publishers would like to thank the following for their
invaluable help: Dave Richards (manager) and players from the
Junior Bournemouth Bobcats, Dorset, England.